The Basic Essentials of
DESERT SURVIVAL

D1737990

by Dave Ganci

Illustrations by
Devon Wick

ICS BOOKS, Inc.
Merrillville, Indiana

Printed in the U.S.A.
All ICS titles are printed on 50% recycled paper from pre-consumer waste. All sheets are processed without using acid.

Published by:
ICS BOOKS, Inc
1370 E. 86th Place
Merrillville, IN 46410
800-541-7323

TABLE OF CONTENTS

INTRODUCTION

Most of the world waited for seven days and nights in September of 1969 to learn the fate of Bishop James Pike who, with his wife, became lost in the Desert of Judah. They were en route in a Ford Cortina to visit the Qumran Wilderness, site of the discovery of the famed Dead Sea Scrolls.

At one point, the Pikes left the main road and became stuck in rough and rocky terrain. The time was 2:45 p.m. on Monday, September 1. The temperature was approximately 130°F (55°C) with a low humidity factor.

The Pikes decided to try to free the vehicle by digging out from under the stuck wheel. They worked until 4:00 p.m. In that one hour and fifteen minutes in 130°F (55°C) heat, in the direct sun, with the ground temperature about 180°F and the heat generated from their own work—they each lost approximately 4.2 quarts (3.97 liters) of water. That's right, over one gallon of water or 7.2 pounds (3.26 kilograms) of body weight. The only liquid they had in the car was two cans of Coca-Cola. They had no opener, so they opened the cans with a tool and lost one third of each in the process.

At this time, 4:00 p.m., they both felt dizzy and exhausted. They rested briefly, then left the vehicle and started walking, looking for help. They took nothing with them. Mr. Pike took his shirt off, thinking this would cool him. At this point, with over a gallon lost from their systems, all organs of their body would have been effected—including the brain and its ability to think rationally. They walked until 6:00 p.m. over rough and difficult, rocky terrain which required climbing up and down washes. Between 4:00 p.m. and 6:00 p.m. the temperature was 125°F (51°C). It was figured that climbing through rock washes, uncovered in that temperature resulted in the loss of about four more quarts of water. At that time the Pikes were experiencing dizziness, headaches, walking difficulties, indistinct speech, decreased blood volume and decreased blood-oxygen content.

v

Mr. Pike was exhausted and had to stop. Mrs. Pike continued and walked into the night. The air temperature cooled and Mrs. Pike pushed on until 2:30 a.m. Tuesday, totally exhausted and disoriented. At one point she fell down and cut her elbow severely. She tried to drink the blood, but there was none escaping. She then experienced depersonalization (felt outside of herself) and was almost insensitive to pain. She came across a road, fell down again and began rolling downhill, cutting and bruising herself. She lay there until 4:00 a.m. when she heard voices of a Bedouin tribe. She was rescued and recovered enough to tell authorities what had happened. A helicopter search for Mr. Pike began at 10:15 a.m. on Tuesday. The air search found nothing and received no signals.

At 1:00 p.m., three hundred men began a search in jeeps and trucks and found nothing. The air temperature reached 140°F (59°) that day. An hour later the searchers found the abandoned car and started following the Pikes' tracks. At 3:30 p.m., they found where Mr. and Mrs. Pike had separated and there was evidence that Mr. Pike had continued to walk after the air cooled off. His tracks were difficult to follow over the rocky terrain and, by that time, he had been exposed to eight hours of sun. Nothing else was found that night and the search stopped until the morning of September 3. An all day search produced no results. Temperatures went to 130°F (55°C) and 140°F (60°C).

Thursday, September 4, was another fruitless search day. Friday was the same and the search was called off, Mr. Pike presumed dead by this time.

On Saturday, September 6, some volunteer searchers found a water hole with a pair of undershorts, possibly left as some sort of signal. Mr. Pike had found water, but for some reason had not stopped there but continued to walk. Later that same day, the volunteers found a plastic briefcase floating in a second water hole. Mr. Pike had found yet another water hole; but left it and continued walking, probably out of concern for his wife.

On Sunday, September 7, the body of Mr. Pike was found. The later autopsy placed the time of death to be sometime on Tuesday, September 2, or within 24 hours of the vehicle problem.

THIS IS A PERFECT EXAMPLE OF ALL THE WRONG THINGS BEING DONE IN A DESERT SURVIVAL SITUATION.

Let's go down the basic list of errors and how they could have been avoided, resulting in the saving of Mr. Pike's life and the suffering of Mrs. Pike. Then we'll discuss the basic essentials of desert survival as they could apply to any desert emergency the reader would encounter.

The first thing the Pikes should have done was provision the car with plenty of water, food, and emergency devices to prepare for any desert problems. (The deserts of the Middle East are far more barren and extensive than anything in the United States, and far less populated). The Pikes should not have left the main road and ventured into the unknown. They probably did not keep track of their location and meandering on the map and really didn't know where they were when they got stuck. They had passed camps of workers and Bedouin Arabs but evidently didn't know how to get back to them . . . or after the first exhausting hour and water loss while trying to free the car, they experienced enough mental and psychological stress that they forgot . . . and panicked.

They made the mistake of leaving the vehicle too soon—when that vehicle provided everything for them to be rescued—even without emergency provisions. The first thing any searchers look for is a vehicle because it is much easier to spot from ground or air than a human.

They had a rear-view mirror to signal with—assuming they knew how. They had gasoline, seat cushions, and a spare tire to light a fire for signals. They had radiator water that could have been used for drinking if not contaminated with coolant or too much rust. They had shelter and shade from wind and sun inside the car.

The Pikes hadn't looked for a bumper jack until after they became exhausted from the digging. Then they couldn't figure out how to use it. They thought it wasn't all there but later investigation showed that it was. They should have used the jack to begin with. Had they waited until evening, they perhaps could have freed the car in the cooler air temperature.

Even leaving the car, they could have taken the mirror and radiator water in a container (Coke cans and anything else they could find). They could have set up signal fires with brush, paper, seat covers, and whatever else they had in the car.

They should not have separated after they decided to walk. But by that time, they were certainly not thinking rationally. They should never have left the roadway, even though it was not the main road.

 Mr. Pike should have stayed at the water hole and waited, certainly for the second one. The water he would have drank at these spots would have revived his mental faculties but perhaps that also increased his concern for his wife and gave him false assurance that he could find help.

Mr. Pike had taken off his shirt and thereby subjected himself to the radiant heat of 125°F (52°C)-140°F (60°C) sunlight, at the same time increasing his heat gain and subsequent mental and physical collapse.

The Pikes did not prepare for the possibility that Murphy lurks everywhere and that minor inconveniences can turn into tragedies for the unprepared. The Pike story is an unfortunate example of all the wrong things people can do in unfamiliar situations. It is not a story of a hostile environment. It is an example of how people coming from one type of environment lacked the knowledge to adapt to another environment.

The Pikes were surrounded by Bedouins who lived in that same desert and liked living there. It had been their home for thousands of years. The Pikes were simply unprepared aliens.

The purpose of this book is to prepare you for a desert survival situation like the Pikes'—or any other survival situation that challenges you.

1. DEFINITIONS

Human history is filled with environmental and physical danger—natural and man-made. Humans had to have a positive attitude to move into new territories and environmental unknowns. They lived daily with the weather, seasons and terrain, learning and adapting as they explored and spread out into the far reaches of the globe. Anthropologically speaking, it wasn't that long ago that our ancestors were adapting to every environment on earth—testing, trying new things—risking.

This risk-taking and positive attitude has resulted in modern technology, and along with it a change of lifestyle, habits and values. In industrialized countries, humans have learned to live in the cities with fast transportation and controlled environments. After a few generations of this new kind of adaptation, humans lose the ability to recognize the natural dangers common to outdoor primitive living. They have formed 'comfort zones' of ease and contentment, and any time they get pushed out of that comfort zone, they become afraid and sometimes helpless.

On the other hand, the urban environmental pressures and isolation from the natural world have left an empty space in many lives, and those personalities long for the back country and the chance to 'get back to nature.'

This has led many folks to jump into 'outdoor recreation' pursuits like hiking, backpacking, trail running, wilderness camping, kayaking, ski-touring and mountaineering.

Many times they get out of it just as fast because they expected instant gratification and success. They do not realize that the natural world moves at the same pace it always has—slow by our standards.

Fast transportation allows us to move through many environments quickly without exposing ourselves to the natural changes and adaptations our ancestors experienced.

On foot, we see, hear, smell and feel the changes and potentials dangers that could effect us. In the automobile, we see the landscape as a blur.

When we do venture out into the wilds, it is usually with enough gear to travel the globe. We carry our support systems with us—tents, sleeping bags, gas stoves, kitchen utensils, on and on until we have sixty pounds (27.2 kg) of 'survival' gear.

What happens when you are caught without that gear? When the pickup breaks down on the back road sightseeing tour? On the rushed shortcut? Or when an injury might strand you on the backpack trip? Or when your vehicle gets stuck in the sand? like the Pikes.

Survival education—or as I prefer to call it, Outdoor ATTITUDE, AWARENESS and ADAPTATION education—can prepare you for this eventuality. That's what this book is about

Attitude

Attitude determines everything we do. It sets the tone for our approach to life. It is the psychological or mental outlook towards problem solving. Humans are problem-solving animals. That's what elevates us above all other critters—the ability to use rational thinking to overcome obstacles, adapt to changing environments and avoid enemies. Attitude involves the positive or negative confidence we carry into emergency or 'survival' situations.

Some people are born with a positive attitude towards everything. They could be parachuted into the Gobi desert with nothing but their shorts and would find a way to survive. Others would be dead before they hit the ground. Cultural environment can influence positive and negative attitudes, but the beauty of the human animal is that positive attitude can be learned with practice. This book will help you do that by discussing the processes of ATTITUDE, AWARENESS and ADAPTATION to the outdoor emergency situation in a desert environment.

Survival

The dictionary defines this word to mean—'to live on.' Whenever the word "survival" appears in the title of a book, magazine or newspaper story, it projects an image—or attitude—of man and woman *against* the environment—creating an adversarial, confrontational battleground—with the environment being the bad guy and our hero being the good guy. The sun and heat are out to fry him; the cactus and thorn bushes are out to grab him; the critters are out to eat or poison him. In other words, the environment is hostile. It is man against Nature; conquer of die. It is typical literary license to create drama and infuse human characteristics into inanimate objects. The truth is that there is no hostile environment on earth. . . . only hostile people.

Native humans adapted to, and formed great civilizations in, every corner of the globe. . . . adjusting to hot, cold, wet, dry weather; flat, round, mountainous, jagged terrain; big, small, loud and quiet critters. From the Arctic to the Sahara to the deepest jungles, humans have become AWARE and ADAPTED—not 'survived.'

Fear

Fear is the most basic emotion and promotes negative attitudes. Fear is a natural reaction to the unknown. It leads to doubt, confusion, panic and finally paralysis. Fear is a physical, chemical reaction—measured in the laboratory—over which we have no immediate power. It goes back through four million years of biological evolution. Then, it was a basic survival tool. It allowed our ancestors to either fight the Saber-toothed tiger or run away from it at top speed—'fight or flight'. A natural super-drug called adrenalin pumped up our physical strength, heightened all our senses and blocked our rational decision making abilities in order to respond physically as fast as possible. This system is still in place, but modern man is harmed by this as much as he is helped. In our particular desert survival situation, fear harms us by pushing us into bad decisions rather than rational problem solving. It is what pushed the Pikes out into the desert.

Well, if fear is a biological reaction, how do we neutralize it. First, recognize it. You know it when you feel it. Even if your mind knows it is irrational. Remember when you jumped out of your theatre seat in the movie Jaws? I do. You knew it was just a movie, but the fear made you jump anyway. You maybe even had a hard time going in the ocean for awhile. That's four million years of inherited fear manifesting itself.

When we experience this fear in the unplanned for emergency situation—or 'survival' scenario, we can limit its effect by the following:

Unless there is immediate physical danger, don't act on the fear. Sit down and force the fear out. The laboratory has measured chemical fear reaction and it can last from a few minutes up to eight hours, if there is no willful action to subdue it. Force it out by recognizing it for what it is—an irrational reaction to problem solving.

Force yourself to start putting your thoughts down on paper. Start a diary of the predicament. Make an estimate of the current situation, a list of what resources you have with you, the weather, time of day, what you see, hear, smell and feel about your immediate environment. This forces you to use your rational mind which will start changing the chemical reaction and help push the fear out.

Tell yourself that fear is just in the way and is slowing down the process of rescue. Get mad at the fear. Replace the emotion of fear with anger. Anger is much easier to deal with.

Now replace the anger with the realization that rational, unemotional thought is what's going to get you back to your comfort zone.

Look around your environment and remember that your ancestors lived out in that environment for millions of years. So can you.

Positive attitude is reinforced by AWARENESS, or knowledge. Fear and negative attitudes are usually based on unknowns, ignorance of the facts. By becoming informed or AWARE, we replace the fear and negative attitudes with knowledge of the subject—and then we can deal with problems involving the subject.

The next section of this book deals with AWARENESS of the various aspects of desert survival. With the right ATTITUDE and AWARENESS, we can then ADAPT to whatever situation confronts us by solving problems rationally and returning to our comfort zones.

2. DESERT LOCATIONS

Desert

Just what is a desert anyway? Some see it as a God-forsaken wasteland, fit for only those things that stick, stink or sting. Some see it as a beautiful landscape with endless sunsets and vistas. Others see it as the birthplace of civilization and the center of all the great religions of the world.

Most scientists agree on a physical description as follows:

1. Deserts have less than 10 inches of rainfall (average) annually, providing little surface water.
2. Evapotranspiration takes place—that is more water evaporates into the atmosphere than is collected from rain; the sun sucks the water from the plants and animals as well as the ground.
3. High air and ground temperatures, resulting in great ranges of day and nighttime heat and cold.
4. Potential high winds because there is little vegetation to stop its progress.
5. Sparse vegetation due to low rainfall.
6. Little or no topsoil; mostly sand, rock and mixtures of both.

That's a pretty cold—or hot—description of deserts. They are certainly more than that. They are whatever we discover in them. When we look closely, we see endless subtle varieties of plant and animal life; endless exposed geologic intricacies; endless shape, form and color; endless vistas and dreamscapes; endless opportunities for hope and reflection.

Where are these desert places located anyway?

Locations

North American deserts cover about 500,000 square miles of land area and are usually divided into six main geographic regions (Figure 2-1).

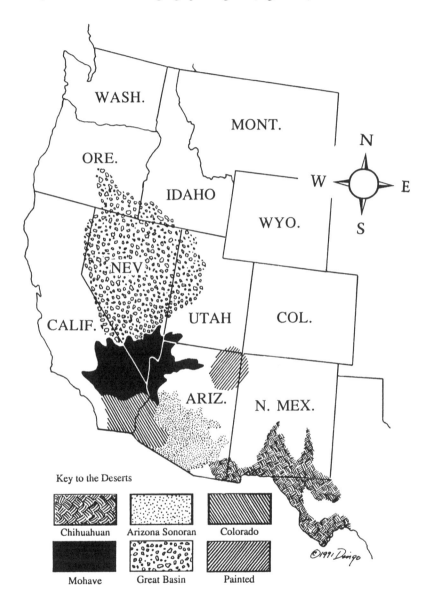

Figure 2-1   North American deserts

The Mohave Desert fills up the southeast corner of California and spreads over into Arizona. Characterized by the Joshua Tree, this desert contains the famed Death Valley. High desert mountain chains jut up off the dry basin floors and many are snow covered in the winter.

The Sonoran Desert covers southern Arizona and extends down into Mexico. It is the 'picture postcard' desert with the lushest vegetation due to its two-season rainfall. The Saguaro, Cholla and Barrel Cactuses characterize this region with the Creosote Bush being the most prominent plant.

The Great Basin Desert is the Sagebrush desert—where that short, scrubby bush with the sweet smell covers hundreds of square miles in all directions. Nevada is almost entirely Great Basin Desert. The region stretches into Utah and northern Arizona. It is a higher elevation desert, therefore cooler in the summer and cold in the winter.

The Chihuahaun Desert extends from Mexico up into southeastern Arizona, New Mexico and Texas. It is similar to the Sonoran but with less plant variety.

The Colorado River Desert, extending along the river on both sides for up to 50-100 miles (80-160 km)or so—is the hottest and driest of the North American deserts with less than 3 inches of rainfall annually. The Painted Desert (Indian country) is in Northeastern Arizona and the Four Corners country of Utah, Colorado and New Mexico.

Another feature of the desert lands is the Riparian Habitat—or the permanent water courses that flow through the dry lands. Normally draining higher, more vegetated regions, removed from the desert lands, these ribbons of life wind through the flat basins on their way to the ocean, most of them emptying into the Colorado River which borders California and Arizona. They are 'exotic' in the sense that they form horizontal oasis where great varieties of plant and animal life thrive along their banks and in their waters. These special life zones extend only a few yards beyond the banks of the water course, then end abruptly and disappear into the dry desert landscape.

These life-giving habitats play an important role in the desert survival scenario if they can be identified. More of that later in the discussion of water.

Let's talk about the weather . . . everyone else does.

Figure 3-1   Winter snow on cactus

Figure 3-2   Summer storm

Figure 3-3   Storm clouds clearing

Figure 3-4   Cactus in bloom

3. DESERT WEATHER

There are some generalities about our weather patterns in the Western deserts, but there are also a lot of unpredictabilities.

Most of our weather comes from the West and Northwest, storm fronts coming from the Pacific Ocean and down from the Pacific Northwest. Some fronts come up from the Gulfs of Mexico and California, mainly in the summer and mainly into the Sonoran Deserts of Arizona and Mexico.

The Western and Northwestern fronts bring clouds, rain, some snow and winds to the deserts in the winter. Anywhere from December to February these fronts can drop much needed moisture onto the dry desert floor. But it's usually less than ten inches—or what's left after the storms have dumped most of their moisture in the higher mountains.

The summer monsoon storms are created by warm, moist air coming up from the two gulfs and combining with the super-heated desert air that rises from the baked ground. This creates huge thunderstorm cells with wild winds, drenching cloud bursts and fantastic lightning displays. These storms provide the summer rains that extend up into Arizona, parts of Utah, Nevada and New Mexico. They don't quite reach the Colorado River, thereby making the area around the river the driest desert in North America with an average of three inches or less of rainfall annually. . . that's dry. Even the lizards carry canteens in this desert.

The winter storms are somewhat predictable, forming measurable fronts with large cloud covers and somewhat uniform rainfall over wide areas. The summer storms are totally unpredictable and broil up in the afternoon so fast you can actually watch the thunderheads form. Thunderstorm cells may be moving across the landscape swiftly or standing still. They can dump an inch or more of water in minutes, then disappear into the evening sky just as fast. They are so sharply defined that it can be raining on one side of the street and dry on the other. These monsoons usually run from late July through early September with the majority of moist Gulf air coming into the States in August/September—creating the humidity that mixes with the hot air temperatures and causing most desert folks to wish they were in Alaska.

What are the dry months in the deserts? The standing joke is that they are all dry—just a few of them are moist. The skies are usually clear and dry from May through the middle of July and from September through November. BUT NOT ALWAYS! Some winter storms can still drop down into the deserts all the way into May. Sometimes they stop in January or barely make an appearance all winter. Sometimes the monsoons start early in June and are over in August. Sometimes we don't even get a winter storm until January.

Spring and Fall are defined by subtle weather changes but mostly by the floral blooms, sweet desert scents and hayfever. The deserts literally come alive in the spring, exploding into colors, aromas and new young critter births.

Fall is also a blooming time for many plants.

So how does the weather effect our desert survival scenario? Glad you asked. Let's talk about the advantages first.

The obvious one is the availability of water, either collected directly from the sky or from runoff. Other advantages are the cooling effect of rain on the body; cooling of the air; shade from the rain clouds.

Disadvantages include flash floods, lightning, too much rain, wind and dust in summer—and hypothermia (too cold) in the winter. Let's talk about these.

Flash floods are common in the summer and can catch the desert traveler snoozing—either in a dry wash just about to turn into a river or at the wheel of the pickup as they ease into what looks like a shallow runoff across the low spot in the road. When the thunderstorms drop huge amounts of water in a small spot, the ground does not absorb that much right away and the resulting runoff screams down shallow washes with vigor and purpose, sweeping everything out of its way, including people and trucks.

Lightning is termed a hazard—like the rattlesnake—but I don't personally know of anyone ever hit or bitten by either. There are some general precautions recommended if on foot when lightning storms threaten—usually in the monsoon season. Stay off mountain summits, ridgelines, open areas, and don't hide under trees or in a cave. What does that leave? Flat ground between trees and on the sides of hills or ridges. I have always just kept on hiking because I think if lightning gets you, the Great Spirit puts your name on it. If a pitcher can get hit on a baseball mound in the middle of a game, it's gonna get you anywhere if it wants to.

For my money there is never too much rain in the desert, and in the summer I look for the thunderstorms and wait to get under them. Summer rain is refreshing to the skin as well as replacement for the chlorine-treated water in most kitchen-filled canteens.

If you don't like rain in any form, most summer thundershowers will pass your given location quickly, leaving pot holes and wet turf that will quickly dry under the 'evapotranspiration' of the sun.

Desert wind and blowing dust can be more of an inconvenience than a hazard. Sometimes visibility is cut short by heavy blowing sand and dirt whipped up from the collapsing thunderstorm clouds. These microbursts can be violent but usually don't last long. They create wind sheer for airplanes and biting sand stings for short-sleeved hikers. They also cause sand-pitted windshields and bare-metal sandblasting on vehicle side panels.

Sit 'em out behind a rock pile or embankment.

Even in the summer, getting soaked in a strong wind can chill the body, especially if the exposure continues into the evening. I recommend a light rain parka in the pack. Also the lightest pair of thermal underwear along with a wool or acrylic pullover hat. These don't weigh much and can provide a margin of comfort for little effort in the event of too much wind and rain in too short a time.

Desert temperatures can vary as much as 80°F (32°C) in one 24 hour period, creating the harshest kind of living environment for all living things. In one May day in the middle of the Grand Canyon it reached 90°F (32°C) at noon, soon to be replaced by a huge late winter storm that swooped over the rim and dumped rain, hail and snow by sundown.

Normal summer temperature ranges reach 120°F (49°C) plus in the southern deserts, dropping to the 70s (21°C) or 80s (27°C) at night. However there are times when the temperature never goes below 100°F (38°C) day and night, usually in July and August. The northern deserts may be slightly cooler during the summer days but can get into the 40s (05°C) and 50s (10°C) at night.

Normal winter temperatures are very comfortable—in the 60s (16°C) and 70s (21°C) with nights getting down to freezing at times in the southern regions; colder in the northern areas. Storm patterns and local topography effect temperatures and humidity.

National weather forecasts can give you a big picture but that's all. Local forecasts are usually spinoffs from the bigger ones and don't tell you much more. Take enough clothing and gear in the vehicle to cover the extremes you think you'll run into. Make your final selection at the departure point, based on forecasts and your observations. With enough experience, you will be making your own predictions, equal to or better than the ones on TV.

Personally, I don't advise people as to when and where they should experience the outdoors. Experience it all, in all kinds of weather. Just learn about it and go prepared. Learn from each experience by keeping notes and photos. Go days and nights; go with folks and alone; just go. If you listen to every safety expert that writes an outdoor book, you will never go anywhere. The important thing is to do your homework and become AWARE of your environment. There is no room for fear or anxiety if you're prepared with the knowledge that allows you to ADAPT, not just survive.

There is an old Mexican saying: "Only gringos and donkeys walk in the noonday sun." The Mexicans have adapted to the desert daytime temperatures by simply sitting—or sleeping—until the late afternoon when the air cools off. They aren't surviving, they are adapting.

The gringos, like the donkeys, bring their stubbornness to the deserts and work right on through the noonday sun.

There are, however, other life forms out there besides gringos and donkeys. How about the native plants and animals?

4. DESERT LIFE

Plants

Most desert plants have adapted over thousands—or millions—of years to the dry, hot climate. The desert areas were once tropical and some plants have changed from much wetter-climate plants into today's cacti and thorn bushes.

What can we learn about survival from them? Actually some basic water conservation principles. Most cacti have shallow, widespread root systems that collect the sparse desert rain quickly,—just after it hits the ground. They suck up as

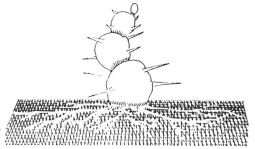

Figure 4-1   Cactus roots

much as they can hold while the gittin' is good. As desert survivors, we will do the same thing if lucky enough to be under rain clouds. We'll spread out our waterproof tarp, plastic garbage bags, plastic sheet, ripped off seat cover, rain poncho—any and all potential water traps. First, we'll dig a hole in the ground as a catch basin, then spread our water-catchers over it and down into it, forming a basin. We'll look around for any trash, bottles, cans, plastic containers and keep them ready to fill. When the rain hits us, we jump into it, get soaking wet, and pull maintenance on all our basins. We become human cacti.

13

Another plant adaptation technique is that of conservation of water. Many plants have waxy outer leaf and bark coverings to slow down the sun's unrelenting attempt to evaporate water from them. Some plants turn their leaves edgewise to the sun all day to limit the surface exposed to evaporation . . . they provide their own shade. Still others simply curl up their leaves, and like the Mexicans, sleep in the noonday sun—unfurling in late afternoon and evening when it gets cooler and the sun's evaporative effect is minimized.

We can learn from the plants. We can cover our bare skin with clothing to minimize evaporation from skin surfaces. We can stay in the shade during the day. And unlike the donkeys, we curl up and sleep during the hot afternoon.

How about plants as food and water sources? Too much has been written (or copied from others) about surviving off the land—most of it written by people who have never done it or never will. Most of us have digestive systems tuned to our civilized menus—grocery store fare. Even if native Americans ate certain wild fruits, nuts and vegetables—it does not mean we can without certain ill effects. I have read books, masters theses and many stories about edible plants; I've talked with native Americans, attended lectures from ethnobotany experts, and spent countless hours experimenting with desert plants on real survival treks. What's my conclusion? Unless you have done the same, forget about eating desert fruits. Unless you have taken a field course and done it yourself, don't experiment in a real survival scenario. Here's why:

1. There are too many variables as to what part of the plant, when, how much and at what time of year they are edible.
2. Even some botanists cannot tell the differences between look-alike edible and non-edible plants.
3. There is little nutritional value in most plants—in the quantity you would be able to eat them.
4. How do you know what your system would do with exotic substances thrown into it? I have been lecturing in the field about Jojoba nuts while popping them down without thinking—then suddenly vomited right in front of the students. Keeping my cool, I simply said, "See what I mean about exotic plants?" I lost an extra pint of water at the same time. That's the last thing you want to do. What if they cause diarrhea—and they have. Then you can loose a couple of quarts (liters) of water and are in real serious trouble.

Leave the 'living off the land' experts to their fantasies. Stick with reality. If you want to experiment with edible plants, do it outside the survival scenario. One of my courses at the Arizona Outdoor Institute consists of three days of hunting and gathering desert plants, where we make a base camp and 'live off the land'—sort of. We prepare some desert foods and mix our experience with real food. We do this in the Spring and early Summer when there are enough fruit, nuts, flowers and seeds to make it worthwhile. But this is a planned desert adaptation and desert appreciation scenario, not the real thing. We have medical backups and are one hour away from a hospital if someone gets sick.

Now, what about acquiring the all-precious water from desert plants. How many pictures and explanations about building a solar still have you seen? How many have you built? How many has the 'expert' who wrote about them built . . . and used . . . over a period of time . . . in what type of soil . . . with what measured results . . . having expended how much sweat and energy in doing so ...? See what I mean? The answer to the above is probably 'one' if any. I know, I've read most the survival books and can tell you how most of the authors got their information. From the U.S. Air Force Survival Manual . . . or they simply copied some previous author who got his information from the Manual.

We have built hundreds of solar stills in all the North American deserts over the years and no two have ever been exactly the same. There are many variables, and again, like the 'living off the land' fantasies, you need to practice the art or you are wasting time and energy . . . and water. Practice at your leisure, or take a course in desert survival and learn how to build a solar still—there are different kinds—but don't count on one to survive.

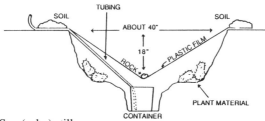

Figure 4-2   Sun (solar) still

We at the Arizona Outdoor Institute have acquired as much as a gallon of water in a still in one day. Know why? Because the soil was so moist from rainfall you could squeeze the water out of the mud. With that kind of soil moisture, there were plenty of open pot holes around full of water that required minimum effort to collect. Why bother with a still? We have also built stills that resulted in no water, or at the most, a cup. Those cost over a gallon of sweat to build. We've experimented with bag stills, tree stills, bush stills, and ground stills. Ninety-five percent of the time they were a waste of energy and resources—mostly water in the form of sweat.

How about plants for shelter? Good idea. If a vehicle is not involved, there are desert trees and bushes in many deserts. When holing up and resting during the afternoon heat, dig out a shallow spot on the north side of the tree or bush. That will be the coolest and most moist spot on the ground. The top layer of dirt will be hot, so scrape it away. Lay your tarp or extra clothing down and snooze away.

Depending on the vegetation in your particular area, bushes and shrubs can be used to create a lean-to or quonset style shelter, creating the all-important shade during the day.

Animals

Desert critters are the subject of many overblown fantasies relating to their potential dangers to humans. There are just as many fantasies dealing with 'edible' animals.

It is a little known fact that more critters can be seen in desert areas than in many other vegetative habitats—mainly in the early mornings and evenings. Why is that? Because there is more open space—less obstruction and cover to hide their searchings and wanderings.

A great variety of insects, birds, reptiles, rodents, and mammals frequent the desert lands. Most of them have adapted to the hot landscape by behavioral— ATTITUDE, if you will—methods, not changes in their physical structure. Like man, they have learned to *escape* the heat. They go underground, stay up in trees, hide inside cooler plants like cacti, burrow under rocks and inside caves during the day. Most desert creatures hunt, mate and have their social gatherings in the evening and nighttime—except, of course, the gringo and donkey.

What can we learn from the critters to apply to our survival problem? Lots of things. After all, when we are in the survival mode, we are just another critter in their environment. We should do most of our moving around at night to conserve water and eliminate heat gain. We can provide shade to lay up during the day—the best of all possible places being a cave. It can be 30°F (1°C) to 40°F (4.4°C) degrees cooler 30 feet (9.144m) inside a cave due to the insulation value between the inside and the outside environments. If there is no cave, the next best place is under a north-facing ledge that overhangs a spot in the shade. That spot never gets the sun, and is always moister and cooler than any other spot on the open desert. It is a microhabitat of cooler soil, cooler rock face and cooler air and it stays that way all day. The third best place is under the previously mentioned plant shade habitat. We obviously can't stay up in trees like the birds or inside Saguaro Cactus trunks like owls, birds and other critters, but we can always take advantage of the plant's shade.

Now, what about critters as 'survival food.' Ha, what a joke, especially without a weapon. Trapping and snaring wild critters looks good on the survival videos and films. Have any idea how long it took to set up the traps and snares? How many were successful? I do; I've tried it. It's a waste of time and energy, better left as a hobby that requires practice and more practice. Food is not your problem in the desert, water is. You can go weeks without food and suffer only minor discomfort.

Poisonous Critters

There is more misinformation and fear concerning biting and stinging critters than all other desert fables combined. The media love to play up these 'bad' guys and create fantasies of danger that don't exist.

Just about every survival book tells the reader to carry a snake bite kit in their first aid pack. Thousands . . . millions have been sold. In all the time I've spent on the desert, and with all the people I have gone out there with . . . and taught, I know of no one who has ever used one . . . including myself.

Speaking of snake bite, let's discuss this much maligned slithering 'bad' guy from the Garden of Eden. One of the slowest moving animals around eats only once every week or so, keeps to himself, is not aggressive unless cornered or protecting young, keeps the rodent population in check and everybody is afraid of him— poisonous or not. They're just critters, trying to make a living like everyone else.

Figure 4-3 Snake coiled

The one most fervently feared is the rattlesnake—we even have missiles named after them. In the desert areas, the Diamond Back, Mohave, Black, Speckled and Sidewinder are out there. You would be lucky to see one, as they avoid humans whenever they can. The Diamond Back and Mohave have similar brown bodies with darker diamond splotches on their backs. The Mohave will be more of a green/brown. Both the snake's rattles will be preceded by white and black stripes. They have flat, triangular heads and will coil when provoked, rattling their tails as warning. The sound is unmistakable. If you run into one by accident, and he coils, simply back away and he will slither in the opposite direction. He has no desire to waste his energy and venom on so large an animal as the human. He is only protecting himself. If, however, you decide to harass the snake, you get what you deserve. Ninety percent of the recorded snakebites reported to the Game and Fish Department are due to someone messing with the snake—teasing it, throwing rocks at it, trying to corner it, pin it down, or catch it, take photos of it closeup, or kill it. The other ten percent were probably doing the same but were too embarrassed to say so. I have spent thousands of hours in the deserts with hundreds of people—day and night—sleeping on the bare ground—and have yet to record a snake bite. A couple of scorpion, ant and bee stings, but no snakes. We've seen them and heard them and left them alone.

Being cold-blooded, they need warmth to operate, therefore they hibernate during the winter, becoming docile and sluggish. They come out in the warm spring and summer and that's when most people see them. They demand respect, not fear.

OK, but just what if one does get bitten? The question is always asked. Ninety-nine out of one hundred chances it will be on the leg or hand. The best thing to do is get away from the snake first. Don't try to catch it, kill it, or bite it back. Don't risk the chance of a second bite from an already excited snake. There is a good chance the first bite did not inject venom. but, the second one might. Normally, if injection of venom occurs, the site will swell and burn quickly. No one ever knows how much venom is involved or how sensitive one is to the venom until it happens.

Squeeze the wound or suck on it, if possible. Clean it, bandage it, then get to the hospital. Don't try to cut it with the snake bite kit razor. Don't try to freeze it with your food-box ice. Don't tie a tourniquet on your limb. Just get to medical help; but, sit down first and get control of the fear. Force the panic out of your system. Remember, fear is a chemical reaction that you can effect by your willpower and confidence. The vast majority of doctors I've talked to, who have treated snake bite victims, say that cut and suck, freezing and tourniquet applications have done more harm than good to bite victims. I agree one hundred percent. Just think about it for a moment. You get zapped by the mad Mohave on the back of the hand. Your adrenalin shoots sky high. Your fear factor is off the charts. You are shaking like a leaf. Now you are going to pull apart that snake bite kit, get that tiny razor out and actually cut incisions right over the two punctures. A physician *trains* to do this— and you are now going to operate on yourself when you can't even hold the razor straight? Forget it. Just try to calm down and determine your fastest way to the hospital without running or pushing too hard. Get your heartbeat back down to normal and remember that more people suffer extreme reactions to bee stings than to all other critter bites and stings combined.

That's right. The honeybee is the most dangerous animal in the wild. Why? Because there are so many of them and all of us have been stung at least once. The law of averages catches up with those who will have an allergic reaction to the bee venom and either die or get sick. And really, are you afraid of bees? So why should you be afraid of snakes or scorpions, or black widows, or brown recluse spiders, or centipedes, or tarantulas or any other smallish critters who file claim to the desert landscape. They are just a part of the system that we had nothing to do with inventing.

The scorpion sting produced a numbing sensation in everyone I know, including myself, who has been stung; nothing more. There are instances of more severe reactions to sensitive people.

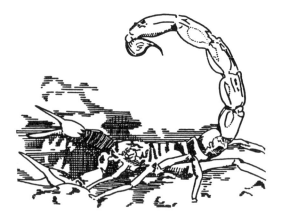

Figure 4-4 Scorpion

I've never met the person stung by a black widow. Most black widow sightings are in the home or in the garage anyway. They, along with the brown recluse spider, like woodpiles, trash, dump sites, refrigerators, kitchen chairs, bedroom closets and back porches.

Centipedes are rare and I've known no one who has been bitten by one.

The Gila Monster—not much of a monster—is a poisonous lizard who has to chew the poison into the hand after some idiot has stuck his hand into its mouth. These critters are rare and beautiful and you will be extremely lucky to see one. The tarantula—featured in the movie Arachnophobia—is harmless. It only looks threatening because it is big for a spider . . . big and hairy. Kids keep them as pets, letting them run up and down their arms.

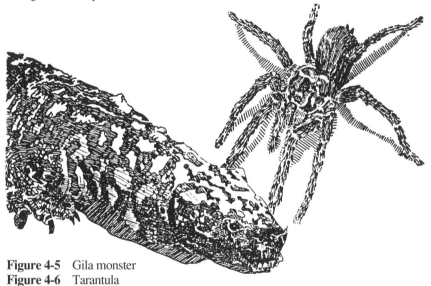

Figure 4-5   Gila monster
Figure 4-6   Tarantula

OK, OK, so the poisonous critters aren't so bad after all. But what precautions should I take to avoid them, you ask? How about common sense and your natural perceptive senses. Ninety-nine out of 100 times you will spot the critter before you get close enough to make him mad. How about at night? Keep your flashlight handy around camp. Most desert critters are out and about at night, but again, they aren't hunting you. You encounter them by accident and carelessness . . . or luck. I personally enjoy the slithery, creeping creatures and admire their ability to survive . . . oops, I mean ADAPT, to the desert environment.

There is no reason to kill any of these critters to 'make it safe.' The next one is just around the corner to fill the niche you have made by dispatching the one you encounter. This includes rattlesnakes. If you are lucky enough to spot a snake, gila monster, centipede or tarantula, just let them go their way and admire their tenacity.

So much for critters. How about us? We're at the top of the food chain. How do we fare out there?

5. HUMANS IN THE DESERT

Case History

Mrs. D. started down the Bright Angel Trail in the Grand Canyon, heading for Phantom Ranch at the bottom—13 trail-miles and 5000 vertical feet away. She was not acclimated to the June desert heat and had done no regular cardiovascular exercise prior to coming to the Canyon.

She left the South Rim at 5:00 a.m., carrying a heavy pack of 60 pounds (27.2 Kg), figuring she would beat the heat to the bottom.

The going was slow due to the heavy pack and lack of conditioning. It took her until noon to get onto the River Trail extension (about 10 miles down) and it was 108°F (42°C).

She suddenly collapsed at this point and went unconscious. Some Boy Scouts came by and tried to revive her by pouring Colorado River water over her. One Scout ran to Phantom Ranch to call the Rangers. The Rangers arrived quickly and continued to pour river water on Mrs. D. while radioing for help.

Paramedics arrived by helicopter in 35 minutes after the patient had collapsed, finding Mrs. D. deeply unconscious and hot to the touch. There was no pulse, little blood pressure and slow breathing. Her skin was pale, eye pupils unresponsive. Her temperature was 105°F (41°C). Physical indications were that Mrs. D. suffered from heat stroke with possible brain and heart damage.

Two IVs went into her as she was flown out to Flagstaff Community Hospital. Her temperature was at 104°F (40°C) when she arrived.

She was given ice baths and massages until her temperature dropped to 99°F (37°C). It was noticed that she had burn marks on her thighs, arms and chest.

On the second day in the hospital, she responded enough to squeeze a hand and blink her eyes on command but could not talk. She started kidney function shutdown and was transferred to Good Samaritan Hospital in Phoenix, by ambulance. Her breathing slowed down again en route and she became unconscious again.

At Good Samaritan, she went on a respirator and underwent kidney dialysis. She was unconscious for fifteen days, then started producing urine and became mentally awake. She stayed in the hospital another fifteen days before being sent home.

Mrs. D. had come close to death and it all happened quite rapidly. One minute she was hiking, the next she had collapsed into a coma and would have died without medical help.

It is surmised that Mrs. D. did all the wrong things through ignorance of the desert environment. First, she probably didn't think of the Grand Canyon as desert because the South Rim isn't. Once she dropped over the rim and started down to Phantom Ranch, she was in the desert. She had descended a vertical mile from the rim to the river and experienced a vegetation and climate variation equal to a horizontal distance of going from Canada to Mexico. She hadn't gotten into physical shape before attempting this vigorous hike. She was carrying too much weight, which compounds heat, and dehydration stress. She didn't drink enough water on the way down. She was wearing black long pants and a nylon shirt. She continued to the river even after feeling exhausted because she was headed for a river trip pickup at Phantom Ranch, and didn't want to miss it.

June is a hot, dry month in the Grand Canyon—the driest, before the summer monsoons get up that way. Few clouds are in the sky and the radiant heat gain is enormous. With little moisture in the air, the sun sucks the liquid out of the skin at a rapid rate. It can happen so fast that the thirst mechanism doesn't catch up and a human can drop from dehydration and not know why. Then nausea can take over and reduce the desire for water even more. People have died of dehydration with full canteens.

Mrs. D's story is the exception and used as an example. However, many heat-stressed people are pulled out of the Grand Canyon every year by Rangers. The Canyon is a testing ground and separates the weak from the strong or the ignorant from the prepared. And what can we learn from Mrs. D's experience? Let's talk about how the human body reacts to heat and dehydration stress.

Heat

Humans are quite limited in their physical characteristics as they relate to desert environments. Some of the limitations are:

a. Humans don't have enough body hair for insulation from radiated heat gain (nor from cold); therefore we need clothing and artificial insulation from both heat and cold.

b. Our skin (outer layer) burns easily; it is very sensitive and fragile, therefore it needs shade, creams, sunglasses, hat, footwear.

c. We require large amounts of water for body functions. Three-quarters of our body is made up of water. We need it for normal functions and for evaporative cooling (sweating), therefore we have to carry extra water with us (externally) and learn to conserve what is already inside us.

d. We cannot endure large amounts of water loss and still function normally, therefore all water lost through elimination of body wastes, breathing and perspiring must be replaced.

e. We cannot endure high body temperatures very long, nor can we store heat like some animals, therefore we need a cooling mechanism called sweating to keep us within the extremely narrow temperature range to survive.

Here's how it all works in the human body:

The normal human body temperature is 98.6°F (37°C)—one or two degrees either side of that reduces body efficiency.

The body can withstand more cold stress than heat stress. If the temperature increases six to eight degrees for any length of time, the body will die. We have all probably suffered a temperature increase of a few degrees at one time or another—that's called a fever. It renders us inoperative. If not reduced, it renders us dead.

The desert environment attempts to raise our body temperature by the following means:

a. Air temperature—If the thermometer reads anything above 90°F (32°C), the human body starts to absorb heat through the skin. The skin temperature is normally cooler than the internal body temperature. As the air temperature approaches and passes 99°F (37°C), the heat gain accelerates and the body temperature starts to rise.

b. Conduction—Heat is gained by the surrounding physical environment such as the ground, rocks, ledges—anything we might come in direct contact with if that object is hotter than about 90°F (32°C).

c. Convection—Hot air blowing against the skin. A slight wind in 105°F air temperature is like standing in front of an air heater.

d. Radiation—Direct sun rays on the skin. That is why it is cooler to the skin in the shade than in the sun. The air temperature is the same as in the shade—but not the radiant heat.

e. Metabolism—Our own body heat is generated by work of the internal organs, especially the muscles. The harder we work (move), the more heat we generate.

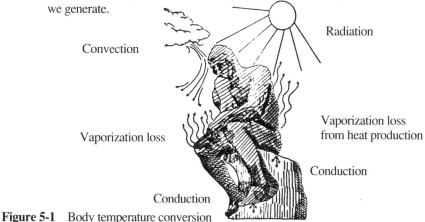

Figure 5-1   Body temperature conversion

All this heat gain is telling skin sensors that something must be done because the body is starting to overheat. Nerve impulses from the sensors relay this message to the hypothalamus organ in the brain. This organ is a temperature-regulating mechanism that immediately sends messages to the heart to start pumping blood to the now expanding arterial system at a faster pace. The same message dilates the blood vessels all the way to the capillaries close to the skin surface. The message starts the fluid flow from the sweat glands, also close to the surface. The flow, consisting mostly of water, a little salt and minuscule amounts of potassium, calcium, and other trace elements pours out onto the skin surface. The air evaporates the liquid, causing an extremely cool temperature gradient. This cools the skin surface and therefore the blood that is now closer to the surface, sending it back to the heart and other organs, cooling them down also. The more heat gain, the more need for sweat on the skin surface.

A good analogy to how the human body adapts to heat stress is the desert water bag. Fill a canvass water bag and a solid canteen with water and hang them both in the sun. When the air temperature reaches 110°F (43°C), the water in the 'sweating' desert bag will be 70°F (21°C) due to the slow leaking surface that evaporates on the bag surface and cools the water. The water in the solid canteen will be 110 F.

The following symptoms and remedies are common in desert heat emergencies.

I. Mild heat injuries
    A Symptoms
        1. Heat Cramps
            a) Caused mainly by loss of salt from the body
            b) Moderate to severe muscle cramps in legs, arms,
                or abdomen, are symptoms.
        2. Heat Exhaustion
            a) Caused by large loss of water from the body
            b) Headache, excessive sweating, weakness,
                dizziness and cramps are symptoms
            c. Skin is pale, moist, cold and clammy
            d. Should be treated immediately by a medic.
    B. First aid for mild heat injuries
        1. Create shade for patient.
        2. Have him lie down.
        3. Loosen his clothing and sprinkle him with water.
        4. Fan the patient to cool him.
        5. Give him water from a canteen.
        6. Let him drink small amounts of water every 3 minutes.
        7. Call a medic immediately.
II. Heat Stroke (a medical emergency)—a severe heat injury caused by an extreme loss ofwater. The patient has lost the ability to cool his body. He may die if not cooled immediately.

A. Symptoms
   1. Sweat stops forming and skin feels hot and dry.
   2. Headaches and dizziness.
   3. Fast pulse
   4. Nausea and vomiting
   5. Mental confusion leading to unconsciousness.
B. First aid for heat stroke
   1. Immediately send for medic
   2. Create shade and move patient under it.
   3. If possible, get him off the ground (about 18" or 45cm)
   4. Loosen his clothing.
   5. Immediately pour water on him
   6. Fan the patient
   7. Massage arms, legs, and body
   8. Cool him off; do not use ice (it may cause shock.)
   9. Evacuate him to aid station ASAP
   10. If he regains consciousness, let him drink small
       amounts of water every 3 minutes.

Cold

Does it get cold in the desert? You bet it does. Due to the tremendous temperature variations in desert lands, days can be warm and nights can get down to freezing. Why is this peculiar to desert lands? The sparse vegetation does not keep the daytime heat trapped in the soil and surrounding air—like more vegetated environments. The heat re-radiates back out into the sky at night, cooling everything down. But that usually takes most of the night to happen and the temperature often doesn't cool off until after midnight.

Winter storms can change the scene dramatically and snow can fall in the desert from early November to May.

We gain cold in the reverse way we gain heat. We simply lose the heat of our bodies to the surrounding environment.

Here's how it happens:

Air temperature: If the outside air is below, say about 60°F (16°C)—we start to feel cool. The skin sensors are telling us that internal body heat will not keep us warm any longer. We must help by putting on some insulation—clothing. The air is sucking the heat from the body.

Conduction: Anything cold we touch, sit, or lie on, sucks more heat from us. Another reason we wear footwear and gloves.

Convection: Probably the most insidious heat thief. Cool wind blowing across the body, especially if it is wet, causes super evaporation and super cooling.

Radiation: Now, radiation is our friend and we welcome the sun's rays. We would like it to warm our skin directly, but the air temperature forces us to leave our clothing layers on. The sun does, however, warm the clothing—thereby adding to the insulation.

Metabolism: Work helps keep us warm by internal energy production. It also means we must feed this production with more food and drink. And if we don't have the water, we are back to square one as far as desert survival is concerned.

Now the skin sensors are telling the hypothalamus to constrict the blood vessels and limit the blood flow to the extremities, causing our fingers, toes, ears, and noses to get cold. This constricting keeps the inner body core warm at the expense of the extremities. The heart, lungs, liver, etc. are much more important than the fingers and toes.

Dehydration

Heat stress is one thing; dehydration (continued water loss without its replacement) is another thing. Dehydration can occur in both hot and cold weather. It is quite insidious and can impair humans in physical stress activities without their realizing what is happening to them.

Water is a biological imperative down to the cellular level. There is no substitute for it, no getting used to being without it and no drug to alleviate the problems caused by its absence in the human body. It is life.

In the desert heat we said that the only way the body can cool itself is to put out water on the skin to be evaporated. Every drop of perspiration is a drop that is lost from some other bodily function, necessary for its efficient operation. Sweat is a diversion of water in an emergency, to be used to cool the body. To maintain efficiency, the body must replace that water or continue to deteriorate in efficiency and eventually become impaired to the point of collapse.

Scientifically controlled experiments on men working in hot deserts have given us some figures on loss of efficiency compared to the percent of dehydration or loss of body water. A man who has lost 2.5 percent of his body weight by sweating (about 1.5 quarts or 1.42 liters of water in 1/2 hour of work in 110°F (43°C) will lose 25 percent of his working efficiency.

When you start losing water that you cannot replace, the blood thickens and the heart has to work harder to pump it around. Everything slows down, including mental capacity—especially mental capacity—specifically judgment, upon which all your actions will depend. Therefore, it can begin to happen without recognizing it. That's why we must learn to recognize the symptoms of dehydration as soon as possible in a survival situation. Oh, sure, you say, "That's easy." Thirst will tell me when to drink. Well, maybe yes, maybe no. The thirst mechanism is still a mystery and sometimes—many times—it fools us. It can come and go. It can be overwhelming and it can disappear. There are other signs of dehydration just as significant.

Fatigue, headaches, nausea, mental confusion, grouchiness, lackadaisical attitude, dry mouth—these are all symptoms. But the one field test most relied on is that of urine color. Normal color is light yellow. As the body dehydrates, the color darkens to deeper yellow, orangish and then brown. Overhydration, or too much water, is passed off as almost clear liquid. So, when you see your urine turning a dark yellow, whether you are thirsty or not, it is time to drink a quart of water.

Most people drink enough liquid only with meals. In hot climates, they become dehydrated between meals. They may feel tired and listless and blame it on the heat when many times it is due to temporary dehydration.

Efficiency lost by dehydration is quickly restored by drinking water. Replacing water lost by sweating will quickly restore a man who is water deficient. It happens in minutes.

We have discovered people on our Arizona Outdoor Institute Desert Survival Courses who have become fatigued without being thirsty. They had full canteens of water. We made them drink a quart. In minutes they were up and ready to go. We made them drink the other quart. They were back to normal quickly.

There is no evidence that anyone can acclimatize to dehydration. Some men have been dehydrated fifteen or twenty times under experimental conditions. It took just as much water to bring them back to normal efficiency after the last dehydration as it did after the first.

If you are in the desert survival situation, and have plenty of water, drink as much as you want when you want it. If you are not thirsty, keep checking your urine color. If you see it changing for the darker—drink water, don't wait for thirst. This is what will keep you one hundred percent efficient. And that's what you want to be for as long as possible because that will allow you to make better decisions and plans for your escape or rescue. These rules are now used in the U.S. Military—they are called 'forced drinking.' The small unit commander will visually inspect the men's urine color and will force them to drink every hour. Sounds radical, I know, but this has been proven an effective method to ensure one hundred percent efficiency on the battlefield.

Here is a fairly normal progression of serious dehydration symptoms: thirst and discomfort; slowing down; appetite loss; sleepiness; body temperature starts to escalate, nausea. At this point, you may have lost three quarts of water. Continued deterioration results in dizziness, headaches, breathing difficulty, tingling in arms and legs, cotton mouth, indistinct speech, inability to walk, tunnel vision, depersonalization, collapse and unconsciousness. These symptoms will occur in combinations and in random order, but almost all of them will become apparent. Again, the thirst mechanism can break down anywhere along the line. So forced drinking may be necessary if you recognize these symptoms in yourself or anyone else.

Alcohol, urine, blood, gasoline, salt water—all these water substitutes will increase dehydration because they require more water to eliminate than they retain. However, slightly brackish water will produce a net gain.

Recent studies have shown that salt, other than what you get in normal food intake, is not needed in the short-term survival scenario. In fact, without plenty of water available to accompany it, salt will further dehydrate you. Don't believe it? Try eating a bag of potato chips when you are really thirsty.

Here are a few guidelines to determine how much water you need to maintain efficiency in the desert. You must realize that just sitting in the shade in an air temperature over 100°F (37°C) will result in continued water loss. The usual figure thrown out is that the human body needs 1 gallon of water per day in the over 100°F (37°C) heat. One or two quarts per day will not keep you efficient and may lead to collapse. I've seen exceptions and have done with less myself, but with great impairment, especially if much movement is required. If the air temperature is above 105°F (41°C) there is a geometric downward spiral of heat stress. At 110°F (43°C) to 130°F (55°C) water deprivation becomes disastrous.

As we saw in the Pike story, one gallon of water can be lost in 1.25 hours— doing all the wrong things, in the worst possible heat.

Always take at least a five-gallon (20 liter) container of extra water in the vehicle when desert travelling. For extensive back-country travel, I recommend ten gallons.

Remember, no matter how hot it gets, if you have water, you can function. Efficiency will drop according to the increase in air temperature, but you can still function. Now, the big question ... What if you don't have much water? What now?

This is the worst of all scenarios—like the Pikes. Now you have to conserve the water that's inside. You have to eliminate as many heat gain factors as possible. Remember our discussion on heat. You must keep the sweating to a minimum.

Keep the body covered, especially the neck and head areas. Keep off the ground if possible. Stay in the shade. Do your work at night or early mornings. Don't conserve the outside water you have. That is false economics. You must stay as efficient as possible until the water is gone. Drink the external water. Ration the sweat, not the water.

Dehydration in Cold Temperatures

Perhaps even more insidious than hot weather dehydration, cold weather water loss fools the human body more. The thirst mechanism is more erratic because of the cold. It does not tell us when we need to drink. This has been proven over and over again by the failure and misery of many winter mountaineering expeditions. Simple lack of water intake has caused many a plan to go awry. Cold weather dehydration reduces the desire for food which causes fatigue which causes psychological defeat which causes inaction which causes more dehydration. Liquids must be forced in the winter as well as in the summer. Again, urine color is the key, especially in cold weather. If the urine is dark yellow, you are a thirsty fellow. If it starts turning brown, you might as well sit down. If you drink and make it clear, you'll be a man of good cheer.

If you don't have water in the colder desert survival situation, the same water principles apply as to the hot desert. You need not eat if you don't have water. The body does not care if it's hot or cold—it still needs water to work efficiently. Water is still the number one priority.

6. WATER

Like every other method of environmental observation, the place to get the best view is from the high ground. Find the highest promontory in your immediate area, even if it's a small one. Take out the binoculars and start a 360 degree scan. Here's what to look for:

Windmills. They may be active or inactive, but there is a good chance you will find water in their holding wells. Mark their location on your map.

Mine sites. What looks out of place? Straight lines and perfect circles do not occur in the natural landscape. What colors are out of place? What scars and scrapes? Mine sites stand out dramatically and are possible water sources, as many old mines were abandoned because drillers hit water and got flooded out. Is there bright green vegetation around the mine scar? Mark this site on your map.

Green vegetation that stands out. This may indicate water at the surface or close to the surface. Plants like Cottonwood, Willow, Tamarisk, Mesquite Tree clusters and Bermuda Grass may indicate a mini-oasis. These plants are not desert plants but have grown there due to ground water closer to the surface. This may also indicate a riparian habitat or permanent stream.

Reflections. These can indicate water, metal, plastic, or possibly shiny rock. Might be worth investigating depending on perceived distance away. Water reflections could be stock ponds, windmill ponds, cattle tanks, rock depressions containing water, spring or seep sights which would also have green vegetation, stream bed water surfacing, mine site water, knocked over and exposed outhouse. You don't know until you investigate. You still mark them on the map and estimate distance.

29

soups on

OASIS

Figure 6-1 A reflection?

Pipeline. Could be a pipeline from a spring to a ranch or cattle tank. Certainly worth a look.

Cattle and cattle tracks. The bovines go to water in the morning and evening. Usually their trails will converge toward water and disperse away from water, but not always. The question is which way are they going, to or from? You may have to investigate.

Vertical rock faces. Water can collect at the bases of these rock walls and usuasly green vegetation will give it away.

Bedrock in stream beds or gulleys. Rainwater collects in tinajas, or water pockets formed on top of rock layers that have been exposed by erosion. They are worth a look.

Bird concentrations. Birds will hang around seeps and springs and any desert water source. If they are spotted in a flock perched in a desert tree or bush, they may have found water for you.

Stream channels. Look for muddy spots, green vegetation, low areas with heavy brush.

Green spots on the sides of cliffs. Could be water seeps where plants are growing.

Dump sites. Could be containers filled with water from the last rains.

In our desert survival course, we find water in all these locations.

You will have to determine the effort required to get to any of the sites, remembering that you will lose water getting there. Make your plans to get up early a.m. and leave before dawn, taking advantage of all the coolness you can. Just before dawn is the coolest it's going to get that day.

Hopefully you have brought some sort of water purification source with you. What are they? The following chart sums up the techniques.

Table 6-1. Water purification Techniques

WATER DISINFECTION: First Step. If the water is visibly dirty or cloudy, strain the water through a cloth to filter out debris or organic matter before proceeding to disinfect the water.

METHOD I: Boil the Water. Water which is maintained at a rapid boil for about 10 minutes should be safe to drink

METHOD II: Chlorinate the Water. Water can be chlorinated using either Halazone™ tablets or common bleach. If Halazone™ is used, an unopened bottle should be used for each trip. Halazone™ must be protected from the heat and from exposure to the air or it will become ineffective. Follow the directions on the label for use. Common bleach is a useful alternative. First, read the label to find out the percentage of chlorine in the bleach; then, use according to the chart below. Liquid chlorine laundry bleach usually has 4% to 6% available chlorine.

Available Chlorine	Drops* To Be Added Per Quart or Liter	
	Clear Water	Cold or Cloudy Water**
1%	10	20
4-6%	2	4
7-10%	1	2
Unknown	10	20

Mix thoroughly by stirring or shaking water in container and let stand for 30 minutes. A slight chlorine odor should be detectable in the water; if not, repeat the dosage and let stand for an additional 15 minutes before using. The water should then be safe to drink.
* 1 drop = 0.05 ml
** Very turbid or very cold water may require prolonged contact time; let stand up to several hours or even overnight.

METHOD III: Iodinate the Water. Water can be iodinated using Globaline™ tablets, tincture of iodine, or iodine crystals. If Globaline™ is used, an unopened bottle should be used for each trip. Globaline™ must be protected from heat and from exposure to the air, or it will become ineffective. Follow directions for use on the Globaline™ label.

If tincture of iodine is used, follow these instructions:

Tincture of Iodine	Drops* To Be Added Per Quart or Liter	
	Clear Water	Cold or Cloudy Water**
2%	5	10

Mix thoroughly by stirring or shaking water in container and let stand for 30 minutes.
* 1 drop = 0.05 ml
** Very turbid or very cold water may require prolonged contact time; let stand up to several hours or even overnight.
If iodine crystals are used, the Kahn-Visscher (KV) method is useful, but requires some advance preparation compared with other methods.

    A. Place 4 to 8 grams (about 1/4 ounce) of USP grade resublimed iodine in a 1-ounce clear GLASS bottle with a leakproof cap (crystals are available from pharmacies in New Mexico, but they may have to be ordered as few pharmacies keep them in stock).

    B. Whenever you want to purify water, follow these steps:

        1. Fill the 1-ounce bottle with water and shake it strongly for one minute.

        2. Hold the bottle upright until the heavy iodine crystals settle to the bottom. The liquid is now a saturated iodine solution.

        3. Determine the proper volume of the saturated iodine solution which must be added to each liter or quart of water according to the following chart, which takes the temperature of the water into consideration.

Water Temperature	Volume of Saturated Iodine Solution To Be Added	Capfuls of Solution To Be Added
3 C (37 F)	20 cc	8-10
20 C (68 F)	13 cc	5-6
25 C (77 F)	12.5 cc	5
40 C (104 F)	10 cc	4

* A single capful from the 1-ounce bottle will contain about
2.5 cc, so the cap can be used as a handy measuring device.

        4. Now, determine the contact time—the amount of time you should wait after adding the saturated iodine solution but before you drink the water; this depends both on the visible cleanliness and the temperature of the water.

Condition of the Water	Recommended Contact Time
Heavily contaminated	at least one hour*
Very cold	at least one hour*
Clean water which is not very cold	30 minutes

* Longer contact times help to ensure better disinfection; several hours or overnight will be very effective.

5. The water should then be safe to drink.

One of the best additions to the survival kit is some kind of flavoring for less-than-tasty water. Kool-Aid, Gator-Aid, Welch's, coffee, tea, sugar—anything you like to help get the water down.

When you find water, no matter what the color, look for critters and plant life growing in it. If they are living in it, you can live on it. Purify it or boil it, then flavor

Figure 6-2   Finding good water…

it. Drink until you are full. Then wait another 20 minutes until your system has absorbed your first tank-up. You will get thirsty again quickly. So tank-up again, wait a few minutes and gulp down another quart to carry in your stomach. You may be uncomfortable at first but you have just bought yourself a half-day's time. You will pass off some of the excess water as clear urine and you will know you are as full of water as you will ever be.

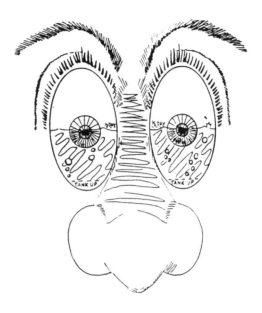

Figure 6-3   Tank up!

What about containers? One, three and five gallon collapsible plastic carriers are best for collecting on the go. Most outdoor stores have good molded plastic containers, holding from a pint to a couple of liters. Take all that you can carry away from the water source.

7. SIGNALLING

The first consideration after calming down is to get signalling devices in place. That is what will get you out of the situation . . . maybe. The last resort will be to walk out, but for now we will try to get rescued.

Signalling simply means getting someone's attention so they will investigate your situation and help you out of it. It means attracting the attention of those looking for you or those who may be passing nearby. You have to create an unusual sight, sound or smell—one that is bright, loud or strong enough to get someone to notice.

Color and motion will attract the would-be rescuer's eyes. Loudness, sharpness and an irritating on-off beat attracts the ears. Smoke smell is about the only aroma signal that will draw attention.

The best colors seen from a distance are orange, red, bright purple and bright white. Your signalling kit should contain a large (9ft. by 12ft.) or bigger tarp with

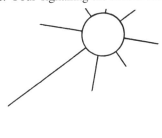

Figure 7-1 Tarps: protect and signal

35

poles and tie-down cord to set up for your vehicle porch and airplane visibility signal. A second color, smaller tarp for waving at aircraft is needed. A Sunday newspaper, kept in the tool box or trunk, can be spread out on the ground in a huge 40 foot X for air spotting. At least three road flares for starting fires and laying out in a 30 foot triangle—if no brush is available for fires—should be carried.

Visual signalling devices

Smoke bombs. Military bombs are best but there are some on the commercial market that are serviceable. If you buy some, try one out before packing them away in your signalling kit.

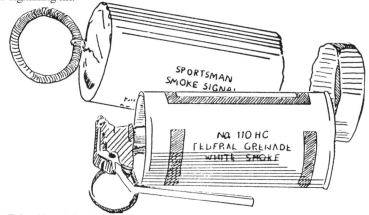

Figure 7-2 Signal device, smoke

Aerial flares. The best are ones shot from a flare gun. The smaller kind, fired with a tube and blank cartridge, are great at night but virtually worthless during the day. They don't put out enough light in sunlight. Carry a few for nighttime.

Fire Starter. Charcoal fire starter is fine, but you can use gasoline. A container must be available, full of fuel and ready to douse the brush piles quickly. When an aircraft is looking for you—or just passing by—you will have seconds to get all your signalling devices going. That requires having everything needed ready including yourself. Be alert to the sounds of aircraft and vehicles.

Signal Mirror. This is the single most important item and should be carried in the personal survival kit when in the hiking mode. But, you must learn to use it and practice with it. The real emergency is not the time to learn. It is a technique and, as such, needs to be practiced in the field with real airplanes. In the Arizona Outdoor Institute Basic Desert Survival Course, we do just that. On the last day of the field trip, a spotter plane comes looking for students in the early morning. Students are required to get the attention of the pilot with their signal mirrors. The pilot will dive at the student, wiggle his wings and acknowledge visual contact. The student holds up a piece of plastic tarp with a number on it. The number is relayed to the instructor and the student is considered 'found and rescued.'

The best mirror is the military Mark 3 Type 2 mirror. There are two sizes of these mirrors. Get the big one.

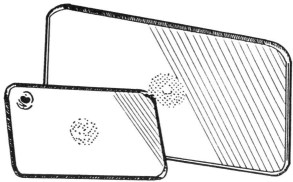

Figure 7-3 Military signal mirror–the single most important tool for your survival kit

If for some reason, you forgot the mirror, other less efficient devices can be used: vehicle rear-view mirror, side mirror, headlight reflector, even shiny hubcaps. The side of a polished bolo knife has been used. Anything shiny and reflective is a potential signal mirror. But, again, unless you have practiced with them, they are like the solar still—good conversation pieces and survival book entries.

Fire. Signal fires will attract attention if bright enough and long-lasting enough. Here's how to build them: After putting on your heavy leather gloves, gather dead brush, wood, cactus skeletons and anything else that will burn. Make three large piles of debris in a triangle with about 30 feet on each side. Place these at least 10 yards from the vehicle. Build them up to head-high if possible. Place crumpled newspaper in the middle of each pile for quick starting. Have your fire-starter ready and handy. Have signal flares or zippos ready. When an aircraft is heard, determine if it is flying low or if it's too high and is obviously en route to a destination. If the aircraft is circling or flying patterns, it's a good sign that it's looking for something—perhaps you. Wait until it is headed your way. Then start the fires, wave the small tarp from the top of your truck cab, and hope the pilot sees the large 'X' laid out on the ground.

Signal Codes. Forget the elaborate code lettering you see on the eternal survival signal card; it has been copied so many times it should be outlawed. All you need is a large X, at least 40 feet long, the get attention. That Sunday paper can be laid out, securing it with rocks and dirt.

Dust. If you have no signalling devices along, you can throw dirt up in the air if an aircraft approaches. That creates dust and if the aircraft is between you and the sun, it might catch the glint of the dust particles.

Nighttime. All lights can be seen further at night—signal fires, flares, flashlight and vehicle lights, taken loose from their molding and turned upward when aircraft approaches. A large, strong-beamed light should be part of your signal kit. The pen-flares are good at night, military flares even better. Any light movement, like waving flashlights or flares will catch attention.

Smoke. Visual smoke signals carry a long way, and it is the one signal that can be kept going all day if burning material is available. Black smoke is more easily seen than white during the day. Oil, rubber mats, tubes and tires make black smoke, but you have to get them started first with a hot burning coal-bed.

Figure 7-4   Creative signalling

White smoke is produced by burning plant material and sprinkling with water. It's not as good as black smoke, but better than nothing.

Smoke smell also carries a long way and is another reason to keep a fire going all day if possible. This requires extensive gathering and should be done before sundown.

Sound Signalling Devices

Vehicle horn. This should be used when another vehicle or persons on foot are spotted—close enough to hear the horn. It should be used in three bursts with two seconds between bursts so the sound doesn't run together. Three of anything is the universal distress signal. Give three bursts, wait 30 seconds and give another three bursts. Continue until either heard or targets disappear.

Whistle. A brass police whistle is best (plastic can break and melt). The same three bursts apply when targets approach. Keep the whistle on a cord around your neck.

Weapons. Gun shots in bursts of three also can be heard from a distance, but are often mistaken for hunters or target shooters. Three bursts, again with two seconds between is best. Try to wait until the target is close so that after attention is gained, you can wave the small tarp and perhaps reach them by voice.

Voice. This is the weakest of all sound signals and should be saved until contact is made by other means. Shouting can make you hoarse quickly and prolonged shouting can take you voice away completely.

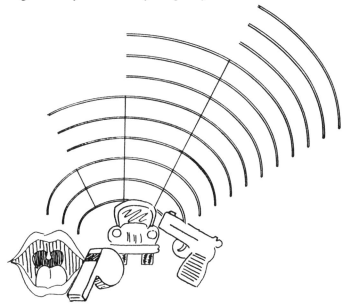

Figure 7-5   Comparative distances of sound signals

Other Signalling Devices

Extra clothing, towels, tarps, tents, aluminum foil, garbage—extra anything that will look out of place can be spread out on the ground to attract attention.

Tie the small tarp onto a Saguaro rib to wave back and forth at rescuers.

If carrying paint, make "X's" and circles on the car hood and top.

Remember that anything involving sight, sound, smell and motion that is not part of the environment will be noticed.

8. DESERT PARAPHERNALIA

Clothing

There are some general guidelines to hot weather clothing and then there are personal preferences. The goal is to remain as cool as possible with the minimum of water loss through sweating. Let's start at the top and work our way down.

The Head. The most important area needing protection. The head should be covered by a hat with a brim and some ventilation. A straw hat is ideal, but will usually self-destruct in a short time. Cotton or canvas with lots of ventilation holes is OK. Tie strings will keep the thing from flying off your head in the wind. Light color is best, but an orange or red one can be seen from above or from a distance.

Neck. A bandanna paper-clipped or pinned to the back of the hat will give needed neck protection. The neck and head areas are particularly susceptible to heat gain and loss.

Face. Sunglasses are a must. They cut glare and eye strain. Keep an extra pair in the glove compartment to replace the ones you will inevitably sit on.

Face cream protection can save a lot of misery. So can lip balm, especially with increased dehydration. As the skin dries, it cracks, then bleeds, causing unneeded stress. Direct sunlight on the skin can dry, burn, and crack the surface; so can reflection off the light-colored desert floor.

Upper body and arms. Take lessons from the desert Bedouins. Wear loose-fitting cotton clothing that allows air to flow around the body. Long sleeves keep the sun off. Make it light cotton, not heavy work clothes type that will trap heat next to the skin and prevent necessary evaporation. The lighter the color, the more sun reflected away from the body. The most efficient system is one that allows enough sweat evaporation to cool the body but no more than that. Direct sunlight on the body would cause radiated heat gain and more sweat would be necessary to counteract that gain.

41

Lower body. Pretty much the same as upper body; loose, light and airy, covering all skin areas.

Feet. A lot of personal preference here since footwear is so critical to comfort and travel. In general, after working with thousands of students, the Arizona Outdoor Institute recommends lightweight but sturdy hiking boots—boots that will withstand the scraping and scuffing of hard desert soils and tough underbrush. Soles should be thick enough and sturdy enough to handle sharp rocks and boulder hopping and provide adequate insulation from ground heat. Running shoes and tennis shoes are not recommended due to lack of foot support and insulation. A soft rubber sole is recommended over hard rubber for comfort and ease of travel. After the hat, the footwear is the single most important item of protection. In many ways, footwear is the most important because you can't go anywhere without it.

Socks are personal preference. We have found wool and synthetic mixes to be best and most durable. Some folks like an inner liner, some don't. The inner liner should not be cotton because it balls up when it gets wet. The new polypropelene materials wick sweat away from the foot into the outer layer sock. Carry two pair into the desert.

Underwear. Underwear? None of my business, right? Well, perhaps so, but a couple of suggestions. Cotton will eventually chafe when mixed with sweat, causing extreme agitation. Light synthetics and especially silk, will not chafe as much and will be much more comfortable on a long desert trek.

Warm nights. Shorts and T-shirts are OK at night because they are cooler and there is no radiant heat gain.

Cold nights. Yeah, what about the cold? Here, we've been talking about heat all this time. Carry a light pair of thermal underwear, heavy socks, wool or synthetic pullover hat and light wind parka. These weigh very little but are very efficient insulators. In the colder, higher deserts, heavier underwear, sweaters or jackets and even sleeping bags should be kept in the vehicle for unplanned bivouacs.

Food

There seems to be more misinformation, hype, silliness and just plain dishonesty regarding this subject than any other topic besides love and war. Everybody seems to know what's best for everybody else, but nobody really knows anything except that if you starve long enough you will die. We, at AOI have experimented with every kind of diet we could think of, including no diet and no food, to test human efficiency in survival stress situations.

In our Basic Desert Survival course we go three days and nights without food and measure our physical and mental responses. No one has yet to suffer ill effects from this. Ninety-five percent of the students struggle through the first day and night, then start ADAPTING. The body tries everything possible to make them miserable when the stomach lacks food. Hunger, headaches, anger, crankiness, nausea, and general discomfort are usually apparent in the first 24 to 36 hours. The body wants food in it but then backs off and starts adapting by using other means of energy production. It simply decides that if it isn't going to get food, it will start using its emergency energy supply—fat. Soooo . . . the body starts losing weight. It also makes its owner start to feel better by decreasing the gnawing hunger and headaches and general lousy feeling. It is transitioning from food to fat and a small amount of muscle tissue, but mainly fat.

By the third day, renewed energy is experienced by the body due to the new survival diet. Most students experience a 'high' and gain renewed enthusiasm and confidence in the course. They realize they have much more inside than they thought. It is at this point that most people accept the survival scenario as a challenge, not a tragedy, and their positive attitude increases dramatically. This is assuming that water is available.

The lesson here is that food is not a problem in the average desert survival situation. All energies should be directed toward finding and conserving water, providing shelter and preparing for rescue.

Survival Kit

The following list is taken from the AOI course outline and is what students carry into the field training exercise. Everything except the clothing and blanket can be carried in a day-hiker or large fanny pack. But that is the AOI kit. Your job is to get out there, get some experience in the desert boondocks, and make up your own survival kit according to your own needs and perceptions. What you carry is all relative to how many conveniences you want to take along.

Desert Survival
Student Gear List

Shorts or loose long pants
Loose long-sleeved shirt with pockets
Long underwear
Sweater
Wool hat
Hiking boots and socks
Tube tent or tarp
Wool blanket or poncho liner
Brimmed light hat
Sun glasses
Sun screen
Chapstick
Bandanna
Field glasses
Day hike pack or fanny pack
Comb
Tweezers
Water purification tablets
Flavoring
Band-aids
Iodine
Adhesive tape
Aspirin

Rubberbands
Flashlight and extra batteries
Whistle
Matches and Zippo™
Water containers (2 to 4 quart)
Food?
Plastic tubes
Baggies
Field knife
Pocket knife

9. DESERT FOOT TRAVEL

In the true desert survival situation it may become necessary to find your way back to the highway, ranch house, or some form of civilization. Either you didn't leave your travel plans with relatives or friends—and searchers have no idea where you might be—or they are searching in the general area and just can't find you. You could be down to your last two quarts of water and be unable to find any in your immediate area. You could be forced to backtrack in hopes of finding water and/or civilization. A multitude of things must be weighed and decided: What is the air temperature? How much strength do you have? Do you want to travel all night? At what pace? Can you hear any signs of civilization—highway sounds, farm or ranch machinery? How well do you remember the route in to where you are? Did you keep track of road junctions, dwellings, cattle guards and fences, mileage? How many miles do you estimate you are from the last civilization? How many miles an hour will you walk? What will you take with you? If others are with you, will you take them or leave them behind? What shape are they in? What instructions will you leave with them if they stay? Are they prepared to signal if they see aircraft or vehicles? If so, can they direct searchers to your route of travel? Will you lose recognition of landmarks if you travel at night.? Can you navigate at night without a compass? Do you know how to find the north star using the Big Dipper and Casiopeia constellations? Can you judge distances at night? What if you have to sleep out before you reach help? How cold will it get at night? Will you spend time looking for water on the way? What kind of signalling device will you take with you? Will there be a turnaround point at which you will go back to your stranded vehicle? How much food—if you have any—will you take with you? If you have a weapon, will you take it or leave it? Who will you call if you reach a phone? How will you direct them to your vehicle if others are waiting there for you?

Other questions will come up to you, the reader. Put them down and contemplate the choices.

One of the most important aspects of foot travel is estimation of distances. Note the following guidelines:

Estimation of Distances

It is important to be able to judge distances when you are making an overland trip, particularly when the journey involves many detours. Not only should you keep an accurate account of distance, but of time travelled also.

For the average person, walking at a comfortable rate, a pace of thirty inches (76.2 cm) traveled over flat country will result in a speed of about three miles per hour (4.8 km/hr.). If you want to get more accurate, count the paces to 100 or 200. If you can measure on a map how far you travelled in the 200 paces, you can get the idea of what kind of time and distance you are walking. To record a long distance, put ten pebbles in one pocket. Transfer one pebble to the other pocket every 100 right foot paces. For a thirty-inch pace (76.2 c.), one thousand right-foot steps will equal one mile (1.6 kilometer), requiring ten pebbles to the mile.

Distances are very often found to have been under-estimated when judged before starting out and over-estimated when judged while your trip is in progress and upon becoming fatigued. When judging distances ahead of you by eye, certain conditions will cause over-estimation of distances, while others will result in under-estimation:

Objects look much nearer than they actually are when:

Looking up or down hill.
There is a bright light on the object.
Looking across water, snow or flat sand.
The air is clear.

Objects look much farther away than they actually are when:

The light is poor.
The color of the object blends with the background.
The object is at the end of a long avenue of vision.
You are looking over undulating ground.

In judging distances, the following table will be useful:

At 50 yards. The mouth and eyes of a person can be clearly distinguished.
At 100 yards. The eyes appear as dots.
At 200 yards. The general details of clothing can be distinguished.
At 300 yards. Faces can be seen.
At 500 yards. Colors of clothing can be distinguished.
At 800 yards. A man looks like a post.
At 1 mile. The trunks of large trees can be seen.
At 2.5 miles. Chimneys and windows can be distinguished.
At 6 miles. Windmills and large houses are recognized.
At 9 miles. An average church steeple can be seen

10. VEHICLES IN THE DESERT

More people get into desert survival situations because of vehicle breakdown than for any other reason. They are out sight-seeing and decide to take the dirt road out to those pinnacles that don't seem 'that far away.' They decide to take a short cut between towns and the dirt road looks good when they first get on it. Halfway across the map the road gets bad and they push on, not wanting to turn back and lose time. Instead, they lose the tierod. They may be simply on their way to a desert camping or hiking spot and the extra heat stress finally blows out the radiator. You know how Murphy works. He waits for the worst possible time to do his work.

Well, let's narrow Murphy's opportunities and do some preparation. Let's become AWARE of the needs of a vehicle once it leaves the pavement and ventures out onto that 'Devil's Highway.'

The first problem is one that most people make for themselves. It's called 'too much in too little time'. They attempt to go too far with the available time and resources for the average weekend jaunt. That translates into going too fast and taking too many chances, giving Murphy ample room to slow you to a stop. We are all wishful thinkers, wanting to do more than is ever possible in the shortest amount of time. Make your desert travel plans with the idea of going slow and seeing more. The purpose of recreation is to escape from the stresses of speed and anxiety, not create more. Slow down and enjoy more. Plan a trip that allows 30% of the time for just loafing.

Traveling on back roads should force the driver to slow down. Speed is the worst enemy of the dirt road driver, just as it is of the highway speeder. Most vehicles that get stuck, do so because they didn't see the obstacle: mud, sand, tree, rut, high center, dropoff, wash, flash flood, soft shoulder, sharp rocks, elephant in the road or whatever—didn't see it in time to stop before the encounter.

47

Many vehicles get stuck while turning around to go back. They pull too far off the road and get the back tires mired in mud, sand, gulleys. Solution? Have one person get out and guide the driver.

Before crossing a wash, check it out for deep sand, sand-covered mud and deep holes.

Is your back-country map accurate or out of date? It doesn't take long for old dirt roads to wash out, for new roads to be cut, for old signs to disappear. It behooves one to check with land-management agencies that have jurisdiction over the proposed route. They would normally have the latest information about the area. Follow the map as you travel. Keep track of the turnoffs, forks, buildings, washes, hills, mileages, time, anything that can be identified on the maps. The idea is to know where you are on the map at all times. If you do that, you are never lost. Even if you break down, you will at least know how far it is to the highway, that ranch house, that well, that cattle tank, road junction or elephant farm.

Getting stuck in sand or mud is the most prevalent form of vehicle stoppage out in the desert boondocks. Precautions include the following: two jacks—one axle and one large bumper; 2-foot square plywood jack pads along with a couple thick carpet squares of the same size; a tow chain and a couple of blocks of wood that will fit under deep-stuck tires; long-handled shovel; spark-plug type pumps or air canisters; cross-bar lug wrench—not the angled kind; come-along winch with metal stake for brake.

When tires are stuck in sand or mud, they will just keep spinning with increased power to the wheels. They must be jacked up and solid footing put beneath them. Use rocks, brush, wood blocks, carpet, anything to give 'grab' to the tires. Don't try to power out. Go easy and slow and let the tires get a grip on the supports. Have every available hand pushing from behind when you put it in gear. Build a pathway for the other tires out of brush, small stones, etc., to give all wheels better traction.

Other common vehicle problems include:

Vapor Lock. When the fuel line is too hot, the fuel turns to vapor between the fuel pump and the carburetor. The engine will turn over but won't start. Try wrapping wet rags around the fuel line—or anything else that will drain off heat from the line.

Flat Tires. Carry two mounted spares with proper pressure. Heavy duty tires for off-highway use are great insurance policies.

Extra Gas. Yes, it happens to the best of us, especially if we get lost and have to go 40 miles further than planned. Carry an extra five gallon can on the outside of the vehicle.

Punctured fuel, oil or transmission pan. That's tough but there are solutions. I have used a screw with a rubber washer formed from a backpack strap, wood plugs, gum and tape.

Cooling system problems. These are prevalent too, usually due to a dirty circulation system or a small radiator for the vehicle in hot country. At least five gallons of water should be in the vehicle, duck tape for quick hose repairs also remember a can of stop leak for radiator leaks. Summer coolant additives are a must.

Take the thermostat out to prevent water flow blockage. A smart desert driver takes an extra, full-charged battery. Electrical problems are also common due to overheating, so the main thing is to keep from running up the temperature gauge.

Certain other tools should be part of your desert vehicle survival plan. Here's a list:

Road flares
Jumper Cables
Axe
Fan Belts
Large Light (2)
Extra Oil and Transmission Fluid
First Aid Kit
Utility Wire
Tool Box

Many modern vehicles carry CB radios now. You can contact a 'good buddy' trucker or other vehicle when stranded, if the battery is operating. But the stuck pickup may be too far out in the boonies or behind too many hills for the CB to be helpful. Don't rely on it! Plan on getting yourself out if Murphy still finds a way to put you in the survival mode.

Be advised that if stuck in the middle of July, you can lose a lot of water—just like the Pikes—if you have to dig a vehicle out in 110°F (44°C) heat. It's OK as long as you have plenty of extra water. If you don't, you had better wait until sundown or you may find yourself reaching for this book and reading the Bishop Pike story.

11. ADAPTING—THE REAL THING

So there you are, alone, with the pickup truck radiator steaming from a split in its side. You are out in the Chocolate Mountains in the middle of the Colorado River Desert in July. It is 110°F (43°C) and you are standing on the sand, which is 170 F, staring at the truck disbelievingly. You really wanted to get to that old abandoned mine site. A light desert wind picks up, pushing the 110°F (43°C) air against your bare arms. It is noon and the sun is beaming down on you neck, head and face. You go stomping around the dead pickup, shouting obscenities, raising your body temperature even more.

You feel better, but you know you need to calm down and start thinking. You get back in the truck, sit down and let the anger/anxiety subside so that you can make some rational estimates of your situation and some sensible plans for rescue.

The radiator has ignored your cursing and it's split all the way down the side. You can't fix that out here. You make up your mind to ADAPT to the situation and accept the inconvenience.

Let's see, where is your location on the map? How far have you come from the highway? What do you have in the pickup? How much food, water, tools, signalling devices etc.

You've been keeping track of road junctions, mileages and signs of past habitation. You're about 30 miles (48.3 km) from the highway, with one gallon of water, lunch of a ham sandwich, boiled eggs and a twinkie, plus one quart of thermos coffee. Oh yeah, that half-pint of Brandy is still stuck under the seat, but forget that . . . for now.

Time to start a diary and list of all resources in the truck. Then think about when you last ate and drank liquids and how hungry and thirsty you are right now. In other words, determine a starting point both physically and psychologically for what

51

has to be a quick ADAPTATION to the natural environment (some might call it 'survival').

Break out the orange tarp and set it up, reaching from the pickup body to the two Saguaro rib poles you found nearby. Put on the straw hat and pin on the bandanna. Open the truck hood and both doors—for ventilation and as a signal of vehicle trouble. Being slightly thirsty, down one quart of water and save the lunch for later, in the cool of the evening. Put on the heavy leather gloves to protect against spines, thorns and angry scorpions, and start collecting brush and dead wood. Form the three piles of debris and stuff the crumpled newspaper in each pile. Stack some creosote bush next to each pile to provide heavy white smoke when the time comes.

Figure 11-1   Creosote bush, detail

Get out the rubber floor mats, the spare tire and the rubber trunk mat for the slow-burning black-smoke fire you'll start immediately. Spread out the Sunday newspaper into the big 40 foot (12.2 meters) 'X', holding the sheets down with dirt and rocks. Pour some of the gasoline out of the extra five gallon can into the #10 coffee can and have it ready to light the piles. Get out the road flares and have one ready to strike for a lighter. Keep the Zippo™ in the pocket ready as backup. Keep the signal mirror and whistle on cords around the neck for quick access in case a plane or vehicle approaches. Attach the small piece of purple tarp to another Saguaro rib and have it leaning against the truck for quick waving. Unbolt the truck seat and set it on the ground under the tarp—which is facing north, providing the coolest angle possible.

You've prepared for signalling. Now take a break on the truck seat and start writing again. The next big question will be, "What's in my immediate territory?" Just like any critter in the wild—now that you are one—you need to take stock of your surroundings. Let's see, ya need to get to that small hill for an observation point—that 'high' point to allow for the farthest reconnaissance. But it's 4:00 p.m. and still hot. Better wait until about 6:00 p.m. when the air temperature has cooled enough to minimize sweat loss in the recon effort . . . *ZZZZZ*.

The chattering of a cactus wren awakens you. It's 5:45 p.m. You're already adapting—just like the Mexicans. Now break out the binoculars and head up the small hill. Remember your notebook, map, pen. Oh, oh. . . you forgot to bring the compass from home. Oh well, the sun is setting in the west; I know when I face it, my right arm is pointing north. From the summit view, make a 360 degree map of the area as far as you can see. What's out there you can use? What direction? How far? Any of the water signs? Habitation? Vehicles? Smoke? Power lines? Fences? Fighting elephants? You notice a reflection off to the side of the road you came in on. It's hard to tell how far away it is because of the normal desert haze—whipped up by the prevailing southwest wind. Notice the broken down barbed wire fencing along the road, the black dots that might be dwellings way off in the distance. Mark it all down on the map Wait! What's that? Sounds like a plane. Scan the sky. It is a plane and heading in this general direction, but angling east.

You rush down the hill, picking up some cholla cactus stems that stick to the outside of your boot. So what? Gotta get those signals working. Throw on the gas, rub that flare to get it started, light the piles, get the signal mirror out.

The plane is now heading away from you and the sun, making the mirror angle extremely difficult to use—the best angle is when the plane is between the mirror and the sun. The plane keeps going away. You grab the hand-made flag and frantically wave it. No use, the plane flies out of sight, the piles are burning out, the sun is going down and so is your morale . . . but don't let that happen. Get busy again and collect more brush before the sun disappears. Now you slip the comb under the remaining cholla spines that cling to your boot and pop them off. The few remaining solo spines are pulled out with tweezers.

You're hungry and want that sandwich since you haven't eaten since morning. But you have only three quarts of water left and no immediate prospect of more, except that distant reflection you saw earlier. Forget the food. You know you can go without it, even though it will be uncomfortable. Keep the fire smoldering with the rubber mats so you can start the three new piles quickly if another plane or a vehicle approaches during the night.

Snoozing fitfully, you are awakened by distant coyote howls. You think, "Boy, what a survivor that canine is." In spite of all-out attempts to eradicate the desert dog, the coyote has spread out from Alaska to South America,in many instances moving into the niche once occupied by the wolf. Most game experts describe the coyote as the smartest animal on four feet sometimes smarter than those on two feet. Why is that? Because of their ability to ADAPT to changing circumstances and the seeming ability to pass knowledge on to their young. Coyotes eat anything, live anywhere, and make fun of men's attempts to kill them off. What can we learn from this critter?

Dawn comes slowly and you have decided you will become like the desert dog and survive, mo matter what. The situation looks a bit grim with only three quarts of water and another 110°F day ahead and airplanes few and far between and no vehicles and hey, quit complaining. Every day above ground is a good day so let's maximize this one. Your only option now is to wait this day out in the shade, be ready for rescue signals and if nothing happens, make a night move toward the highway.

You berate yourself for not leaving a note at home, telling your wife where you were going, other than 'exploring.' Should have left a detailed itinerary and stuck to it. Then, after 24 hours, search teams would know where to look. Oh well, too late for that.

The day drags on and you get bored. Why not practice a little direction finding. Let's see, without a compass, we can use a wrist watch. Point the hour hand at the sun. A line drawn halfway between the hour hand and 12:00 o'clock—clockwise—points north (figure 11-2). The tops of the barrel cactus tend to point south or southwest. At about noon, with the sun directly overhead, it angles a little bit off the vertical, pointing south.

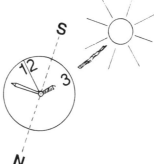

Figure 11-2   A watch for a compass

A few planes fly over too far away and you think you hear a couple vehicles but they are only insects buzzing into your imagination. Two quarts of water are downed. One left. The hunger pangs are starting to go away and so are your options. Tonight is the night. You must travel.

The sun disappears but the heat remains as the baked earth tries to give off some of its accumulated daytime heat. The rocks are still too hot to touch and the ground too hot to sit on. The air temperature is cooling faster than the surrounding terrain, so you must wait awhile to make your move. Tuhe idea is to move at a pace that does not increase perspiration. Conservation of water is the key tactic.

The day-hiker is packed with all your survival items, including the stale lunch in case you find water. Two notes—one on the inside and one on the outside—are placed on the pickup windshield, giving your time, date and direction of travel and hopeful destination—the highway. The smoke-fire is put out. It's 9:00 p.m. and time to move. One more survey from the hilltop to see if any lights are apparent. There are far-away lights toward the highway and you can still see the reflection of the would-be water hole under the bright desert starlight.

Moving out at 9:30 p.m. and heading back down the dirt road you came in on, you figure your normal stride is about two miles an hour. With 30 miles (48.3 kilometers) to go to the highway, theoretically it should take you about 15 hours. Ha, on one quart of water? What will your pace be in ten miles? That reflection will be the key.

The Big Dipper comes up and you find the North Star by extending a line out from the two end dipper-cup stars to the next brightest star—Polaris. Later, the Big W constellation (Cassiopeia) can be used also (figure 11-3). You stuffed three road flares into the day-hiker to use with the pen flares, should an aircraft pass close. You don't use the flashlight. It's not needed to walk on the road and it kills night vision.

Figure 11-3 Star navigation

Psychological ADAPTATION must be applied at this point. It is easy to slip into night 'day-dreaming' and random reminiscing. You must keep mentally alert for all possibilities of water, habitation, other vehicles and approaching aircraft. Nighttime hiking can create its own world and you must avoid this. Your head must be on a swivel, just like the coyote's, to absorb everything around you as you travel. Hearing becomes as important as sight due to limited nighttime visibility. By attentive listening, you might catch the sounds of other campers in the vicinity, their vehicles, their laughter.

You notice sweat starting to form under your arms. Slow down. You're moving too fast, too anxious to get out. Keep that water in the body. After walking an hour, you find another small hill and climb up on it for a break. That reflection is closer and you estimate it to be 7 or 8 miles (approx. 12 kilometer) away. It seems to be a short distance from the road, off to the right. The USGS topographic map you're using does not show any water tank along the road, but it is dated 1965, so who knows? Maps lie, especially older ones. The only thing you can really count on not changing are the topographic (elevation) lines, and terrain features. All other things can change.

You feel better at the slower pace and realize you're trucking along at the most efficient pace.

Your mind starts dozing in the monotony of the walk—ZZZZZ. The slight movement on the road snaps you awake. It slithers away from you, heading for the nearest creosote bush. Popping on your headlamp, you follow the critter and stop as the Diamondback coils and gives you her message, 'Back off.' You do, and now resume the walk with a little more adrenalin and alertness.

The plan is to walk 45 minutes then rest ten. The night air is cooling down—almost refreshing—so you pick up the pace a bit. It's going to be a long night.

It's 2:00 a.m. and fatigue is starting to catch up; fatigue caused by dehydration, hunger, lack of sleep, the long walk, tension of the situation. How far is that reflection now? Up on another hill. There it is about 2 miles (3.2 km) away. Still dark, can't see what it is. Think I'll close my eyes.

Yip, Yip, Awoooo! The coyote bark startles you awake. The eastern sky is slightly green. It's nearly 5:00 a.m. Damn. Fell asleep. Two more hours and it will be hot again, and you're still 9 or 10 miles (approximately 15 kilometers) from the highway. You shake your head and look around. That reflection is brighter now. Let's watch it a bit in the growing light. There, yeah, small, bright patches of green around it. Maybe, just maybe. Let's go, but remember to keep the pace moderate. Try not to sweat. Get back on the road again. God, it's thirsty out! Can't wait any longer. Down that last quart of water now. Conserving it won't do any good.

Another hour or so and the sun is peeping over the horizon. You come across that dirt side road coming into the main one. This must lead to the reflection or close to it. Another 100 yards and up the side road and you notice a small berm raised off the desert floor. You can see the tops of some Tamarisk and Willow trees just over the edge. You run up the berm and see it. Beautiful, sparkling, with muddy water, a small water catchment basin. And there next to it a shallow concrete cattle tank with a pipe running into it. This water is all that's left from the last rainfall runoff. You want to stick your head right down in it and drink until you puke. But you can't do that. Settle down and do it right. There's only an inch-deep pool and you want to skim the top without getting sediment. Take the zip-lock baggie out. Spread it open and skim the top of the cattle pond. This way, you can get a pint at a time right off the top and pour it into your container, using your bandanna as a filter. You pop a couple Halazone purification tablets into your 2-quart container, then build a small fire with some brush and the dried, broken bottom branches of the nearby creosote bush. What the hell, it's 6:30 a.m. and time for coffee. You realize now how beat and dehydrated you really are. Your urine is dark yellow and your mouth feels like cotton. It's hard to wait that half-hour for the Halazone to take effect. The water boils and you start sipping coffee after adding a ton of sugar. Almost immediately you feel different. The human body is so adaptable that, with a little consideration, it can snap right back from fatigue to readiness almost instantly when the main deficiency is water.

Break out that squashed ham sandwich. Mmmm, ain't life grand! Time to relax, kick back and let the water and food turn into new energy and enthusiasm for the long hike on out to the highway. What's that? A vehicle coming down the side road toward you. It's a pickup. You wave. The old rancher stops, eyes you up and down, and you tell him your story. He is heading for the highway and you hop in. "Yeaaah," he drawls, "Gotta have an oversize radiator to drive around this desert in the middle of the summer."

You agree, yawn, and doze off.

When you get to the first phone at the restaurant, you call your wife and tell her how to find you. If she has called the Sheriff's Office to notify them of your failure to return, call them immediately to let them know you're OK. Then sit down to some eggs and hash browns, followed by hot cakes and sausages.

As you lean up against the wall in the shade of the restaurant porch, you reach down into the bottom of the day-hiker and pull out that Brandy…maybe just a nip to celebrate . . . *ZZZZZ.*

EPILOGUE

There are no experts in outdoor survival. There are only students. I am an advanced student because I've been out in the desert lands more than most people. I've also made more mistakes. I've also taken a lot of other people out there in adaptation courses, learning as much from them as they do from me.

The desert is there to enjoy, not fear. The enjoyment will increase dramatically with the gaining of knowledge of the 'lands of little water.' Visit some museums, botanical gardens, zoos. Do some reading. Take a college course in desert natural history. Take a course from one of the outdoor schools listed. Then, get out there and experiment. You will come up with your own assessments and techniques as you learn, and you'll go through some trial and error . . . 'Experiential Education' they call it in the academic world. But who cares? That's part of the fun of it.

Go, go behind the sand dune.
No matter if you find nothing.
The treasure is not there anyway;
it is inside you waiting to be found,
and it cannot be found in one place.

Go, go behind the sand dune,
before the sand dune disappears
or before you vanish
in the mists of obligation,
with no batteries for the flashlight.

Go, go behind the sand dune,
and don't follow the road;
you've been following it all your life.
Go over the top, and if you stop
to look behind, you'll see—nothing.

Go, go behind the sand dune,
You can't untie the knot, you say.
Then cut it, leave it dangle,
wave goodbye to your anchor
and solo walk if you must, but

Go, go behind the sand dune,
and if all you find is loneliness—
that is reward enough
for awhile.

Dave Ganci

APPENDIX 1: OUTDOOR SCHOOLS

Arizona Outdoor Institute
4733 Gloria Drive
Prescott, AZ 86301
(602) 445-9617
Dave Ganci, Director

Tom Brown, Tracker, Inc.
PO Box 173
Asbury, NJ 08802-0173
(201) 852-7826
Tom Brown, Director

Malheur Field Station
HC 72 Box 260
Princeton, OR 97721
(503) 493-2629

Boulder Outdoor Survival School
PO Box 905
Rexburg, ID 83440
(208) 356-7446
Dave Westcott, Director

Reevis Mountain School of Self-Reliance
HC 02, Box 1543
Globe, AZ 85501
Peter Bigfoot, Director

Outward Bound
384 Field Point Rd.
Greenwich, CT 06830
(800) 243-8520

National Outdoor Leadership School
Dept. S, PO Box AA
Lander, WY 82520
(307) 332-6973

APPENDIX 2: REFERENCES

1. Alive In The Desert: the complete guide for desert recreation and survival / Kraus, Joe. Paladin Press, c1978. 113 p. : ISBN: 0873641272 RID: 78-015396

2. The Anza-Borrego Desert Region / Lindsay, Lowell. Wilderness Press, c1978. viii, 165 p. : ISBN: 0911824677: RID: 77-088647

3. At Home In The Desert : surviving and thriving for a day, a week, or a lifetime / Angier, Bradford. Stackpole Books, c1984. x, 144 p., [2] p. of plates : ISBN: 0811721531 (pbk.) RID: 84-000039

4. Backpacking Death Valley / Gebhardt, Chuck. s.n.], c 1975 vi, 134 p.: RID: 75-027630

5. Basic Desert Survival / Dempsey, Jim (James V.) Boy Scouts of America, Theodore Roosevelt Council. 36 p.: RID: wln88-011996

6. A Camper's Desert/ Tucker, Betty J. La Siesta Press, 1971. 36p.: RID: wln75-003220

7. Desert Awareness: information for anyone traveling in the desert southwest/ DARES, c 1975. ii, 34 p.: RID: wln81-02924

8. Desert Hiking/ Ganci, Dave. 2nd ed. Wilderness Press, 1987. xii, 178p.: ISBN: 0899970869 (pbk.) : RID: 87-002209

9. Desert Survival / Nelson, Dick, 1940- 1st ed. Tecolote Press, 1977. [88] p.:
   ISBN: 0915030063 RID: 75-027719

10. The Desert Survival Field Test / Dupree, Louis, 1925- Arctic, Desert,
    Tropic Information Center, Research Studies Institute, Air University,
    1956. iv, 83 p.: RID: wln79-043630

11. Desert Survival Handbook / Lehman, Charles A. Primer Publishers, c1988.
    91 p.: ISBN: 093581034X (pbk.) RID: wln88-073468

12. Member's Handbook For The Desert Trail Association. Desert Trail
    Association. The Association, c1983. 14 p.: RID: wln84-135971

INDEX